# CELTIC MYTHS
## AND BELIEFS

# CELTIC MYTHS
# AND BELIEFS

CHARTWELL
BOOKS, INC.

Published by Chartwell Books
A Division of Book Sales Inc.
114 Northfield Avenue
Edison, New Jersey 08837
USA

0-7858-0997-X

This book is produced by
Quantum Books Ltd
6 Blundell Street
London N7 9BH

Project Manager: Rebecca Kingsley
Project Editor: Judith Millidge
Designer: Wayne Humphries
Editor: Andrew Brown

The material in this publication previously appeared in
*An Introduction to Celtic Mythology*

QUMCG&M
Set in Times
Reproduced in Singapore by United Graphic Ltd
Printed in Singapore by Star Standard Industries (Pte) Ltd

# CONTENTS

# INTRODUCTION

Celtic myths have enthralled listeners and readers for centuries. They conjure up images of moonlit landscapes with white-robed druids performing strange rituals and brewing potions. Without a doubt this view of the Celtic past is itself a myth, colored by eighteenth- and nineteenth-century Romanticism with its love of mist, mystery, and magic. For the Romantic poets and artists the Celtic myths provided a nostalgic escape from the Industrial Age to an era ruled by "nature" and "spirits" and peopled by heroic warriors and fair-skinned maidens.

We, too, require our dreamworlds and the Celts continue to attract us today. Celtic art remains fashionable, particularly in jewelry: It has its own abstract charm, which appears to hold the secrets of an unknown world. Celtic myths and legends weave a similar spell: The storyteller takes us from a world of seemingly real people and transports us to an incredible fantasy land of fairies, wizards, heroes, and monsters; his skill is such that not only we do not notice the transition, but also the fantastic tales seem so believable. It is easy to be bewitched by such a culture. But if we are to learn about Celtic society through its mythology and beliefs we must first of all deconstruct our own modern myth of the Celts.

## WHO WERE THE CELTS?

The Celts were not a single race, but a number of diverse peoples who, despite coming from various ethnic origins, all displayed certain common characteristics. They had sufficient shared features, for example in language, in social and religious institutions, and in their general way of life, to mark them as a distinct nation. The earliest historical references to the Celts occur in Greek literature around 500 BC. By then the Celts had already expanded from their original homeland, which comprised southern Germany and part of Bohemia, and were inhabiting a wide geographical area, ranging from the upper reaches of the Danube in eastern Europe across to France and Spain in the west. Archeological dating of Celtic finds not only confirms the accounts of the ancient Greek writers, but also informs us of the prehistoric Celtic past. We can tell from discovered remains, for example, that a recognizably "proto-Celtic" culture existed around the upper Danube in 1000 BC. However, some archeologists now argue for a widespread and gradual "Celticization" of cultures which already existed in Bronze-Age northern and western Europe: Thus, "Celtic" Britain might be said to date back to as early as 1500 BC, when the so-called Wessex culture had the "heroic" social features which conform with the early Irish Celtic myths.

## THE CELTIC DOMINANCE OF EUROPE

Toward the end of the fifth century BC the eastern European, or "Hallstatt," Celts were exploiting iron for tools and weapons and expanding their territories, firstly across Europe toward France and the Iberian Peninsula, as the early Greek historians affirm. By about 400 BC Celtic tribes had made incursions into Etruscan and Roman Italy, and having almost succeeded in besieging Rome in 387 BC, finally settled in the Po valley. The Celtic culture of this period is known as "La Tène," after a site in Switzerland which

*Left: Celtic god on outer panel of the Gundestrup Cauldron, Denmark (first century BC). This gilt-silver cauldron was found in a bog in Denmark, outside the boundaries of the Celtic world; but its mythological images are undoubtedly Celtic. Here, a colossal god demonstrates his power over men holding wild boars. The boar and pig were sacred animals, often used for important sacrifices; they were also employed as warrior symbols in the form of helmet crests.*

*Above: Etruscan fighting Gauls (Etruscan alabaster funerary urn from Pieve, Italy; fourth century BC). The warriors are represented in an idealized classical Greek manner; the Greeks are distinguished from the Celts by their horses and helmets. The Etruscan language, like ancient Celtic, has only survived in brief inscriptions such as that above the scene.*

It is not clear exactly when Ireland was first occupied by the Celts, but archeological remains show that they were definitely inhabiting the island by the third century BC. These Celtic peoples are described as insular Celts to distinguish them from the continental Celts of mainland Europe.

A further Celtic expansion took place in the fourth century BC and was directed toward southeastern Europe, the Baltic, and western Turkey. We find Alexander the Great receiving Celtic ambassadors at his Macedonian court; and in 279 BC we hear of Celtic tribes attempting to loot the Greek sanctuary at Delphi, defied by a miraculous fall of snow sent by the god Apollo. In the following year Celtic tribes originally from Gaul crossed into Asia Minor and established themselves in the region that still bears the name Galatia. The Greeks distinguished between these oriental Celts, whom they called *Galatoi*, and the Celts of western Europe, whom they called *Keltoi*. The Romans made a further distinction by naming the French Celts *Galli* (Gauls) and the British Celts *Belgae* (originally from what is now Belgium) and *Britanni* (Britons).

## THE FALL OF THE CELTS

Although in the early part of the third century BC the Celts controlled a vast area of Europe, from Galatia in the east to Britain and Ireland in the west, they were ill-equipped to establish an enduring empire or confederation as the Greeks had done and the Romans were about to. They lacked any real form of central organization and, although they shared a common culture, common social and religious customs, common language, and common artistic traditions, they had little sense of cohesion or political unity. They were divided into aristocratic tribes, ruled by

demonstrates typical features of fifth-century BC Celtic society. Many archeologists see La Tène as the first truly Celtic culture, and certainly these are the people referred to from now on as Celts by the classical historians. Their military presence in northern Italy in the late fifth and early fourth centuries BC is attested by Roman mythical accounts of the Gallic siege of Rome, which was apparently frustrated by the warning cackles of sacred geese; and some Etruscan funerary relief sculptures depict battles with Celtic warriors.

By this time most of Britain had also been conquered by the Celts. It is thought that the earliest Celtic immigration into the British Isles occurred in the fifth century BC, another took place in the third century BC, while the final major influx was in the early first century BC.

chieftains who appear to have been constantly fighting one another rather than working together. In some areas the Celts were a ruling minority, surrounded by an often hostile indigenous population. Long distances weakened lines of communication between the Celtic tribes, encouraging further disintegration. By the end of the third century BC the Celts' influence of Europe was in decline. Before long they were being threatened on several sides: in the north by the Germans, in the east by the Dacians, and in the south by the Romans, all of which probably fomented tribal divisions among the Celts to facilitate their own invasions. Within a hundred years no more than a fraction of the former Celtic territories remained under their control. Only in Gaul and Britain did the Celts preserve their independence and their separate identity.

This was not to last long, however. In the first century BC Gaul was invaded by Emperor Julius Caesar, renamed Gallia, and incorporated into the Roman Empire. A century later, in AD 43, Emperor Claudius conquered Britain and renamed it Britannia. Over the next four centuries the Romans steadily destroyed the Celtic civilization in both lands. By the time the Roman Empire collapsed in the fifth century AD the Celtic language in Gaul had been almost wiped out. In Britain the Celts

*Top left: A map of Celtic Britain and Ireland showing tribal territories and key settlements and sites.*

*Bottom left: The extent of the Celtic world from the early Hallstatt era to the period of Celtic dominance in the third century BC.*

had been driven to the furthest extremes of the land: Scotland, Wales, and the southwest of England. When the Roman presence in Britain came to an end at the end of the fifth century, it was followed by that of the Anglo-Saxons. From then on the area of Celtic speech and sovereignty gradually got smaller and smaller. In a bid to escape complete eradication some Celtic tribes emigrated from southwest England and settled in Brittany. Today a modern form of the Celtic language of this period is still spoken in parts of Brittany.

Meanwhile, Celtic Ireland had enjoyed almost complete security from invasion. As a result its culture, traditions, and language, which linguists call Goidelic and which in its modern form is known as Gaelic, survived for much longer than had been the case elsewhere in the Celtic world. In fact the Celtic Irish social order remained virtually intact long after Ireland had officially become a Christian country and Irish adopted as the written language. For this reason Irish myths, more than any other Celtic myths, have preserved the early, prehistoric Celtic culture in vivid detail.

*Left: Roman bronze figure of a Gaulish prisoner (probably from Umbria, Italy: c. first century AD). The prisoner wears the trousers, belted tunic and cloak of Gaulish aristocrat: a practical outfit for horse riding. Irish male and female aristocrats appear to have worn long linen tunics gathered at the waist with decorative belts or girdles; woollen cloaks were also worn. Social status was reflected by the relative richness of color and embroidered decoration on both tunic and cloak. Gold and silver brooches, torcs, and body ornaments would also be worn by high aristocrats.*

## ANCIENT CELTIC SOCIETY

The Celts did not write their own histories. Therefore we have to learn about their civilization from the works of contemporary Greek and Roman writers, such as the Greek geographer Posidonius and Julius Caesar. However, most of these classical authors had no first-hand knowledge of the Celts. Instead, they derived their information from earlier sources, and many of their accounts were based on the assumption that the Celts were uncivilized barbarians. Even Caesar, who had a better opportunity than most to become acquainted with Celtic customs in Gaul, did not rely entirely on his own experience and observation. Classical evidence must therefore be treated with some caution. However, many of the ancient writers' descriptions of the more extreme Celtic customs have been corroborated by archeological discoveries and surviving Irish literature. Archeology has confirmed, for example, that Celts did perform human sacrifice and indulge in head-hunting.

Caesar has given us a reasonably objective account of Celtic behavior and dress in the first century BC. He tells us that the Celts lived in *oppida* or small townships, some of which have been identified with the three thousand or so Iron-Age hill-forts of southern Britain; similar *oppida* existed throughout continental Europe and Galatia. Archeological evidence has allowed reconstructions of the *oppida* dwellings, such as at Butser Hill in Hampshire, England. These were generally circular houses with wooden walls and thatched roofs; the banqueting halls of some of the great Celtic myths would appear to have been rectangular, although this may have been a medieval adaptation of the original stories. Opinions vary among

archeologists as to the exact function of these hill-forts: It is not known for certain whether they were permanent villages or temporary shelters.

The Celts were primarily a warrior society ruled by brave warrior kings, queens, and aristocrats. Their enemies respected them as superb horsemen and fierce, volatile fighters who could ride for miles on end and then fight long and hard. The ease and extent of the Celtic tribes' conquests in Europe demonstrate that at the height of their power they were ruthlessly efficient in war. Both historical accounts and myths reflect the Celtic pride of dressing up for battle. In *Gallic War V* Caesar wrote "The Britons dye themselves with blue woad in order to appear more terrifying in battle. They wear their hair long, and their bodies shaven except for the head and upper lip." Diodorus of Sicily, a contemporary of Caesar, described the Celts as "tall and muscular, with pale skin and blond

*Above: "The Dying Gaul" (Roman marble copy of Hellenistic bronze of the second century BC). The Greek rulers of Pergamon (central Turkey) commemorated their victory over the Galatian Celts with a public monument depicting the defeated enemy. The Romans later copied the figures in marble, probably in celebration of their own victories in Gaul and Britain. The heroic chieftain is readily identified by his Celtic torc, mustache and bristling lime-washed hair.*

*Left: Reconstruction of Iron-Age huts at Butser Hill, Hampshire, England. Archeology has provided evidence of sizes, shapes, and materials used in building Celtic dwellings. The Butser Ancient Farm has also launched experiments with Celtic farm animals, crops, cooking, and pottery methods.*

*Below: Reconstruction of a Celtic temple and sacred enclosure, Hayling Island, Hampshire, England. In the first century BC the sanctuary appears to have been a fairly temporary structure of wood and thatch. Later a more substantial stone building was constructed.*

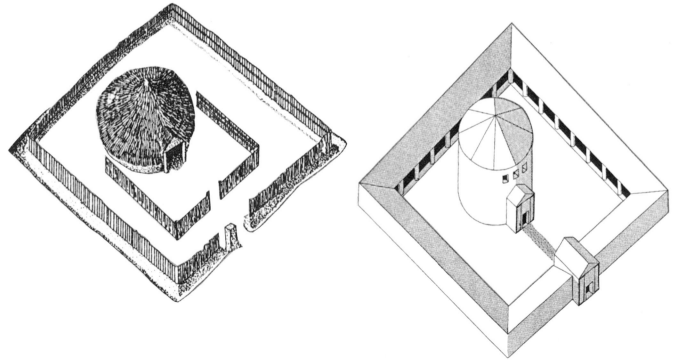

hair which they highlight artificially by washing it in lime-water; they gather it back from the forehead to the top of the head and down to the nape of the neck ... therefore the hair becomes so heavy and coarse that it looks like the mane of horses." Another Roman writer, Herodian, who was writing in the third century AD, added: "As they are not used to clothes, they wear iron ornaments about their waists and necks, which they consider to be both decorative and a sign of wealth ... they tattoo their bodies with abstract patterns and all sorts of animals." Classical marble sculptures showing Celtic soldiers and prisoners conform with these literary stereotypes and archeologists have found tattoos on preserved Celtic flesh.

As well as being excellent warriors, the Celts were also accomplished farmers. They grew corn, cultivating fields on a regular basis with ox-drawn plows instead of manual implements. They also depended on extensive trade, and learned the use of coinage from the Greeks and Romans. As noted by Herodian, the Celts placed great importance

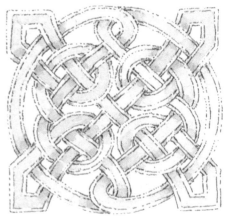

*Right: Bronze helmet with decorated neck-guard (British; first century AD). The Celtic warrior's helmet was often highly decorated depending on his rank. This is a relatively restrained example with decoration in the taut curvilinear La Tène style: however, the holes on the crown might have held a plume or other fixture. Artistic representations of Celtic warriors depict them wearing animal crests, such as birds or boars; horned helmets were also worn.*

*Right: Typical Celtic motif. Celtic artists often decorated jewelry, weapons, and everyday and ritual objects with complex interlacing designs such as this.*

*Right: Cross-legged handle found in the Oseberg ship burial, Norway (c. ninth century AD). The enameled, geometric patterns on the figure's chest are typical of late Celtic Irish art, and the bulging almond-eyes and angular features also betray a Celtic origin. The bucket was probably loot from a Viking raid on Ireland. The figure may represent Cernunnos, whose iconography often portrays the Celtic god of nature, animals, and hunting with crossed legs.*

on visual displays of wealth. This fact is reflected in the eye-catching quality of their art. Celtic artists and craftsmen produced not only some of the most intricate jewelry and the finest ornaments of all the early civilizations, but also some of the most decorative functional and everyday objects, such as buckets, cauldrons, chariots, and some of the most stunning battle dress, including helmets, swords, and shields.

Throughout the Celtic world learning, literature, and religion rested on an organized system of three professional classes: the druids, the bards, and, between these two, an order of soothsayers, known as *vates* in Gaul and *filidhs* in the Irish tradition. An essentially identical system also probably existed in Galatia, too. The druids had the highest social status, being considered semidivine. They conducted a system of education, enforced legal decisions, and officiated at religious ceremonies. The Celts were an intensely religious nation, and worshiped a whole host of gods and goddesses. Their religious rituals played an important role in reinforcing the sacred power of the druids, and in maintaining the social hierarchy of chieftains and tribes. The *vates* carried out many of the druids' functions and in many respects were a subordinate order of the druids. The bards were the class concerned with literature, and appear to have been held in almost equal respect to the druids.

Most of the bards' stories have not survived, for the simple reason that they did not write them down. Instead they relied on memory in the oral tradition. However, we do have some evidence of the subject matter and form of these early expressions of Celtic culture. The Roman writer Ammianus Marcellinus, who wrote in the fourth century AD, stated that the Gallic Celts by that time had become civilized (he meant Romanized) but maintained their own druidic religious philosophy and musical traditions: "The bards celebrated the brave deeds of famous men in epic verse to the accompaniment of the sweet strains of the lyre." Other sources, as well as the later, written versions of the myths themselves, support Ammianus's statement that the bards' stories mainly glorified Celtic heroes, though "epic" and "lyre" were probably Graeco-Roman equivalents for whatever terms the Celts used.

The aristocratic Celts passed their days in hunting and fighting, and their nights in feasting, dancing, and lovemaking. It was during the feasting that the myths and legends of Celtic society were relayed by the bards. Neither the myths nor the classical writers discussed the lower classes of Celtic society. Similarly, they had little to say about Celtic women, except that they were "shared between groups of ten or twelve men." To the Romans and ourselves this would have appeared barbaric, but it may well imply a matriarchal system in which women had the social privilege of a number of lovers. Certainly high-ranking Celtic women enjoyed

*Left: Wayland's Smithy, Chambered long barrow, Oxfordshire, England (c. 3500BC). Wayland was the Norse smith god; legend stated that if a traveller left his horse at the site, together with a coin for payment, the horse would be shod and the money gone when he returned. Such ancient monumental tombs were often mythologized by the celts who, like the later Danes, did not understand their original function.*

a degree of power unknown to their classical counterparts: witness the warrior queen Boudicca, also known as Boadicea, who led her Iceni tribe in a first-century AD rebellion against the Roman invaders. Although we must bear in mind that the Celtic myths were probably always told from a male viewpoint, the human female characters in Celtic mythology are rarely the downtrodden or faceless figures of Greek myths, which might also suggest that, unlike in classical Athens, women formed part of the bard's audience.

The mythical world remained so integral a part of Celtic society that when Christianity arrived, the spoken myths could not be destroyed. Instead, they were often Christianized or given Christian endings: gods became God; the druid priests of the old religion were overcome by the saints of the new religion. The greatest wonder is that any of the myths have survived for so many centuries. These myths are now ours, and we should read, feel, and learn from them, before handing on to the next generation this enchanting window into the rich and varied past of the Celtic world.

*Right: "The Holy Well" (William Orpen, tempera on canvas; 1916). The Irish symbolist artist has depicted the "beehive" huts of a Late Celtic Arran community. The islanders are being converted to Christianity in the waters of their pagan well; Orpen's artist friend Sean Keating stands above the well, apparently unconvinced by the new religion. The deserted crofter's hut in the background and the shamefully naked "Adam and Eve" in the center reinforce Orpen's criticisms of cultural change in Celtic places.*

# The Myths of
# the Celts

*Right: "Culhwch, the King's Son" (tempera on wood by Arthur Joseph Gaskin, 1862–1928). The tale of Culhwch, the legendary son of King Celyddon Wledig, and Olwen is one of the best-known stories from the* Mabinogion *collection of Welsh Celtic myths. It is also one of the earliest tales in which King Arthur appears. The story is rich in British mythical characters, the most significant of whom is Mabon, the Celtic god of youth. Culhwch's quest to free the ancient god might suggest that the original myth reflected a serious religious ritual that involved the symbolic rediscovery of a lost god. Typical Celtic themes in the tale include the jealous stepmother, age-old talking animals, and the freeing of a prisoner. Also of a particularly Celtic nature are the powerful descriptions of the attributes of Culhwch and Olwen.*

Celtic myths have been preserved in two main traditions: Some were recorded by Christian writers, while others have stayed alive in the oral folk traditions of surviving Celtic areas. Gaulish literature, being purely oral, disappeared entirely with Gaulish language: Julius Caesar recorded that the druids of Gaul thought it improper to record their learning in writing. As a result Gaulish mythology is lost beyond recovery. Similarly, there is a lack of material from other former regions of the Celtic world, although Celtic themes can often be observed in European folk-tales. This has resulted in the apparent bias of the myths toward the insular Celts of Britain and Ireland.

### THE SURVIVAL OF CELTIC MYTHOLOGY

The writing down of Irish Celtic literature had already started by the end of the sixth century, but only a few fragments of manuscript survive from the period before AD 1100. The earliest substantial survival of Irish mythology is a manuscript called the *Book of the Dun Cow*. Its Christian writer (author would be the incorrect term, implying an original creation) was a certain Maelmuri, whom historians know was murdered by Viking raiders in his cathedral at Clonmacnois in 1106. The curious title derives from a lost earlier manuscript of the seventh century AD which had been written by St. Ciaran on the hide of his pet cow.

There is evidence to suggest that the Celts in Britain also inherited a rich mythological tradition, although it is poorly documented in comparison to Irish literature. British mythology is now best known from the *Mabinogion*, which was the title given by Lady Charlotte Guest to her 1849 English translation of a collection of eleven Welsh tales preserved in earlier manuscripts: These are the *White Book of Rhydderch* of around 1300–25 and the *Red Book of Hergest* of around 1375–1425. *Mabinogi* means, broadly speaking, "a tale of childhood": this was a mythical account of the conception, birth, and early training of a Celtic hero. Lady Guest's word *Mabinogion* (which she incorrectly thought was the plural form of *Mabinogi*) therefore implied that all eleven tales were of this genre. In fact only the first four tales, or "branches," are from an original *Mabinogi*. They abound in mythological themes, motifs, symbols, and the gods of ancient Britain.

*Above: The mountainous Atlantic coast of Ireland. Landscape description was an essential skill for the Celtic bards: By locating the heroic activities of mythical characters within a recognizable world, myth became reality.*

*Above: "Dierdre of the Sorrows" (black chalk by John Duncan, 1866–1945). The artist has depicted a character from one of the most popular of Celtic love stories. A particularly Celtic feature of the tale is the powerful female characterization of the heroine Deirdre, including her wooing of the hero rather than waiting for his advances. Early cultural links between Scotland and Ireland are reflected in the story.*

## THE NATURE OF CELTIC MYTHOLOGY

Just as the Celts were not a single, united race, but rather various tribes that shared common characteristics, so too their mythology is not a close unity. In fact it is as diverse and varied as the tribes themselves. This perhaps reflects the decentralized structure of the Celtic world, in which each tribe was an independent unit with its own gods and heroes. This has resulted in a mythology which is often described as "local and anarchic." That said,

it is nonetheless true that the Celtic learned classes had a highly developed sense of affinity, based on a common cultural inheritance. Even though Celtic myths had endless narrative variants, and characters of varying names and physical features, the underlying themes were largely constant and common throughout the Celtic world. It is this underlying coherence that allows us to speak of one Celtic mythology rather than several.

It is the Irish tradition that has left us the greatest surviving record of Celtic mythology. The Irish Celts themselves classified their myths by theme: plunderings, battles, voyages, adventures, elopements, etc. But they can also be divided into three broad categories: miscellaneous tales associated with the reigns of various kings, the cycle of the Ulaidh, or "Ulstermen," and finally the cycle of Fionn mac Cumhaill and the roving bands of warriors known as *fiana*. As well as this collection of varied tales, the Celts created a number of pseudohistorical works. Among these is the *Leabhar Gabhála Éireann*, "The Book of the Conquest of Ireland," commonly known as *The Book of Invasions*, which is said to describe the several invasions of Ireland from before the time of the Great Deluge.

The Celtic bards were teachers as well as entertainers, and the behavior of their mythical and legendary characters provided living Celts with ideals, thus ensuring the continuity of the warrior society. Recurrent themes in Celtic mythology can therefore inform us about the preoccupations of their civilization. A love of beauty and bodily display is evident throughout the myths: When warriors go into battle, for example, their brightly colored clothing, glowing jewelry and bristling hair are visual symbols of their heroic status. And heroines signify their own high and leisured status by wearing their hair in time-consuming intricate plaits, and by setting off their white unweathered skin with rich jewelry.

The world of nature was an unexplained and alien place to the Celts: Therefore magical happenings tend to occur outside the stronghold; talking animals and birds feature in many of the stories; and Celtic divinities often represent the forces of nature. It is most likely that some of these stories were originally mythical explanations of religious mysteries or quests. So visits to the Otherworld, for example, might reflect an original rite of passage in which Celts passed from childhood to adulthood by means of a ritual period of absence outside the community. The druidic philosophy encouraged a belief in immortality and the myths celebrate this idea: Love persists beyond the grave in the form of intertwining trees on burial mounds; heads of dead heroes retain supernatural powers. Such beliefs were a consolation to the warrior society, where the hero's greatest glory was to die in battle.

Many elements in the myths appear to mirror an earlier prehistoric "heroic" period of Celtic culture, and thus the Celts of Caesar's day probably viewed their mythical ancestors with as much romantic nostalgia as did their admirers in the nineteenth century. However, the myths also contain legendary representations of real historical characters, such as the fourth-century AD Roman emperor Magnus Maximus, who appears as Macsen Wledig in the *Mabinogion*. This historical example suggests that other mythical figures, though unknown in history, might also have once existed as real persons whose deeds were outstanding enough to have been preserved in both bardic poetry and folk memory.

## THE HEROIC TRADITION

Like all Celtic mythology, ancient Irish literature records the exploits of its warrior heroes. Tribal warfare and individual strength and bravery are its preoccupations. These stories served as an education for young Celtic noblemen, the vivid heroic characters providing them with models of youthful warrior behavior. The most important of the heroic myths was the Ulster cycle which tells of a great conflict between the Ulaidh on the one hand and, on the other, Medb and the Connaughtmen supported by the rest of Ireland. The cycle is heroic literature par excellence and it concerns itself with the activities and virtues that typify all the heroic societies of the Celtic past. It pictures an aristocratic, warrior society with a La Tène culture around the time of the birth of Christ. During this time the Ulaidh were ruled by King Conchobar mac Nessa, who had his royal court at Emuin Machae, near the present city of Armagh. He was the focus of a society of heroes, of whom the most famous was his nephew CuChulainn, the adopted name of a boy originally called Setanta. While the rest of the Ulaidh were struck down by a mysterious illness, CuChulainn bravely defended the Ulster province single-handedly. By engaging in a long series of combats with the opposing army, this youthful warrior held back the Connaught advance until his compatriots had recovered their strength.

The following extracts from the saga of CuChulainn are taken from the twelfth-century manuscript *The Book of the Dun Cow*, the earliest surviving written version of the Ulster heroes. As in the Welsh tale of Pwyll, the storyteller presents his audience with an apparently "real" ancient Celtic world of hill-forts and recognizable place-names. However,

*Above: 'Ossian's Grave': a neolithic grave above Glen Aan, Country Antrim, Ireland (c. 2500BC) The monumental stone graves of earlier cultures were revered as sacred by the celts.*

the "fairy" world is never far away: "real" landmarks, such as New Grange burial mound (Bruig na Boinde), exert their magical influence, heroes are born, and superhuman deeds are performed.

We learn from Fergus, one of the Ulster chieftains and a narrator of the cycle, that CuChulainn's period of initiation into the heroic life began when, as a young boy of six, he made his way alone to his uncle's court at Emuin Machae and succeeded in routing 150 youths reared there for Conchobar's protection. Upon this Conchobar adopted CuChulainn as his own son. Conall, another of the Ulster chieftains, continued the story:

"Conchobar wondered at the feats of his nephew and he asked his men whether CuChulainn would grow into a man and perform similar heroic deeds: they all agreed that this would be so. 'Come with us to the feast of Culann, the blacksmith', said Conchobar.

'I shall finish the games,' replied CuChulainn, 'and follow after you.'

"At the feast, Culann the smith asked his royal guest whether all were present. 'Yes,' answered Conchobar, forgetting his foster-son, 'and we are ready to eat and drink.'

'Well then,' said the smith, 'let us close the doors and make merry; my dog shall guard the cattle in the fields: No man will escape him, for he requires three chains to hold him, and three men on each chain.'

"Meanwhile, the boy was on his way to the feast. As he entered the courtyard of Culann

*Left: "CuChulainn," (John Duncan). Duncan has portrayed the Irish warrior with tartan cloak and late Celtic brooch. The Dundee artist drew on the style and medievalism of the Pre-Raphaelites to create images of Celtic mythological heroes.*

the smith, the dog went for him. The disturbance was heard by Conchobar and his men, and they watched from the windows as CuChulainn fought the dog with his bare hands. He held it by the throat and back and smashed it to pieces against a pillar. CuChulainn was taken into the house. 'I am glad for your mother's sake,' said Culann, 'that you are alive. But that dog protected all my goods, and now I am done for.'

'Fear not,' said CuChulainn, 'I shall raise a puppy of similar pedigree for you, and until it is large enough to guard your property I myself shall be your watchdog.'

'Then we shall call you CuChulainn, "The Hound of Culann," from now on.' said Conall.

"Such were the exploits of a boy of six," said Conall. "What mighty deeds can we expect of him now that he is seventeen?"

The next stage in CuChulainn's initiation was the taking of arms. Having learned from Cathbhadh the druid that whoever takes up arms on this particular day will be famous forever, though short-lived, he went immediately to seek arms of Conchobar, saying: "Provided that my fame lives, I care not if I be on this earth a single day." He broke fifteen sets of weapons before he was finally given those of the king. He then set off on a series of successful warlike exploits against the enemies of Ulster. Later he goes abroad to be trained by the supernatural Scathach, who teaches him skills that render him invincible.

*Right: The Atlantic coast and the ring of Kerry mountains, Ireland. Mild winters encourage continual vegetation throughout the year here; Mediterranean trees grow in some parts.*

**The feast of Bricriu** – Bricriu "Nemthenga" ("Poison-Tongue") invited Conchobar and the Ulstermen to a magnificent feast in a beautiful house designed specially for the occasion. Opposite the house Bricriu built a cottage with large glass windows so that he could see into the house, for he knew that the Ulstermen would not allow him to dine with them.

Before the feast Bricriu visited Loegaire, Conall Cernach, and CuChulainn, three of the greatest heroes of Ulster, and told them of a prize that would be reserved at his feast for the champion of champions: "You will become king of all Ireland," Bricriu told each hero, "if you win the champion's prize. You will receive a cauldron large enough to hold three warriors full of wine. You shall have a boar fed for seven years on milk and grain in the spring, curds and sweet milk in the summer, wheat, and acorns in the autumn, and meat and soup in the winter. And you shall

have a noble cow which for seven years has grazed on heather and milk, meadow-herbs, and corn. And you shall have in addition one hundred large honey-cakes. This is the prize intended for you alone, for you alone are the greatest of the Ulstermen. You are to claim the prize as the feast begins." So Bricriu tempted each hero and returned to finish the preparations for the feast.

The Ulstermen arrived on the day appointed for the feast, and each man and woman took their place in the great hall according to their rank. When all was ready the musicians began to play and Bricriu announced, "Over there is the portion reserved for the champion. May the best man win." And with those words he left the hall and entered his cottage.

As Bricriu had hoped an argument began immediately between Loegaire, Conall Cernach, and CuChulainn, and soon the three warriors were fighting. Conchobar stepped be-

tween them and Senchae, who was the oldest and wisest of the Ulstermen, said, "We should not have fighting during the feast. Tonight the portion shall be divided between all three of you, and tomorrow we shall ask Ailill, King of Connaught, to settle the dispute." All agreed with these words of wisdom and soon the company was merry with food and wine.

The feasting continued but soon the three heroes and their wives began squabbling once more over the champion's prize. It was decided that the three should journey in their chariots to either the King of Munster, Cu Roi, son of Daire, or to Ailill and Medb, King and Queen of Connaught: one of these would settle the dispute. They raced one another westward across the hills and plains toward Connaught and Munster, and the ground shook beneath them.

Medb welcomed the heroes with a vat of water to cool them off and fifty women to attend them in their guest-rooms. They then told Ailill and Medb that they had come to seek their judgment in the dispute over the prize of Bricriu; and all cursed Bricriu for his troublemaking.

Ailill could not make his mind up about the three contestants, so Medb took the judgment upon herself: "There is no difficulty at all in judging them," Medb told her husband, "for Loegaire is as different from Conall Cernach as tawny bronze is from white gold, and Conall Cernach is as different from CuChulainn as white gold is from red gold." She summoned Loegaire: "I consider you to be king of all Ireland," said Medb, "and you are to have the champion's prize; you are to return to Conchobar and the Ulstermen and show them this as a token of our choice." And she gave him a bronze cup, its base decorated with a bird in white gold, and Loegaire

drained the wine in it, and joined his fifty women in bed.

Medb then summoned Conall Cernach, and said the same to him, and gave him a white gold cup with a golden bird on its base. He too drained the wine and went to bed; his fifty women were joined by Sadb Sulbair, daughter of Ailill and Medb.

Finally she summoned CuChulainn, and Ailill joined her in judgement. To the hero was given a cup of red gold, and the bird on its base carved from a priceless gem. "You are champion of champions," said the King and Queen of Connaught, "and your wife Emer is in our opinion the first lady of Ulster. Return to Conchobar tomorrow and claim the prize." CuChulainn was joined in bed by Princess Findabair.

*Below: Round tower at Clonmacnois monastic settlement, Ireland (c. tenth century AD). This Christian settlement was vulnerable to Viking attack: such defensive towers were typical of the early Celtic Christians in Ireland. It was here that* The Book of the Dun Cow, *a rich and early manuscript of Irish myths, was written on the hide of a pet cow.*

The three heroes then bade farewell to Ailill and Medb and the people of the fort of Cruachu and each returned separately to Ulster. Conall Cernach and CuChulainn were held up by various adventures and when they eventually reached Conchobar's fort at Emuin Machae, they found the court in mourning: Loegaire had arrived before them and falsely announced their deaths. The bickering that ensued was halted by Sualtam, father of CuChulainn, who called everyone in for a homecoming feast. "Why not let another hero claim the champion's prize?" said one of the Ulstermen during the merrymaking. "After all, if any of these three had been chosen during their stay at Cruachu, he would have brought home a token as proof." At this challenge Loegaire produced his cup and claimed Bricriu's prize. "The prize is for me," said Conall Cernach, taking out his cup, "for mine is a golden cup and yours is only bronze."

"Then I am the champion of champions," cried CuChulainn, and he showed the company the red-gold cup with its precious-stone bird. "Ailill and Medb have judged," shouted Conchobar and the Ulstermen. "We award you the champion's prize." But Loegaire and Conall Cernach refused to acknowledge the decision and accused CuChulainn of bribing Ailill and Medb. Out came the swords once more. Conchobar stopped the fight and Senchae the Wise pronounced that the three should go to Cu Roi of Munster for his final judgment.

When they reached the fort of Cu Roi, they found that he was away from home, but Blathnat his wife had been instructed to wine and dine them until her husband's return. After dinner Blathnat told the three that each night one of them must take the night-watch, according to Cu Roi's bidding. That night was the turn of Loegaire, for he was the eldest.

The moment the sun had set, they felt the fort revolve like a water-wheel for Cu Roi put a spell on it every night, so that no enemy might find its entrance gate after dark.

Loegaire stood watch while the others slept. As it began to get light, a giant emerged from the ocean in the west. Though he was far away, the giant seemed to Loegaire as tall as the sky. As he advanced, Loegaire noticed huge tree trunks in his fists, which he hurled at Loegaire. They missed their target and the raging giant picked Loegaire up like a baby in his fist and

*Below: Maiden Castle hill-fort, Dorset, England (c. 300 BC). The stronghold of the Durotriges Celtic tribe has a long and complex history, dating from around 2500 BC, but only reaching its present size in the Celtic period. The remarkable winding approach to the main entrance proved little defense when the Romans stormed the fort in the first century AD.*

crushed him as if between two mill-stones. the giant dropped Loegaire over the walls of Cu Roi. When the others found his half-dead body, they thought he had tried to leap the walls as a challenge to the other men.

On the following night it was the turn of Conall Cernach to watch and the same giant caused the same injuries that had befallen Loegaire. The next night was for CuChulainn and it was an evil night, for it had been prophesied that a monster from the lake beneath the

*Below: Warrior fights monster (bronze matrix for making decorative helmets; eighth century* AD). *The Celts decorated their helmets with scenes of power.*
*Here, a warrior with an axe confronts a wild beast.*

citadel would devour all who dwelt there. Just before sunrise there was a great thrashing of water which startled CuChulainn who was half asleep. He looked over the walls and saw the monster, who rose high above the lake. It turned its head and attacked the fort, opening its huge mouth to swallow hut after hut. CuChulainn leapt high into the air, thrusting his arm down the beast's throat and tearing out its heart.

The hero hardly had time to rest before he too saw the giant rising from the ocean. The giant threw his tree trunks and CuChulainn threw his spear: all missed their targets. The giant then tried to grasp CuChulainn in his fist, but CuChulainn was too quick, and he performed his salmon leap and circled the giant with his sword. "I'll give you anything, if you spare my life," said the giant. "I want the champion's prize and Emer to be the first lady of Ulster," said CuChulainn. "Granted!" called the giant as he disappeared into the morning mists.

Cu Roi returned the next day and heard about the great deeds of CuChulainn. He accordingly granted him the prize of champions and the three heroes of Ulster set off for home. And once more Loegaire and Conall Cernach refused CuChulainn the prize, but CuChulainn was weary of the contest and the matter was allowed to rest.

Some time later, Conchobar and the Ulstermen were about to dine at Emuin Machae when a hideous ogre appeared at the door and challenged them to the game of beheading. The three great heroes were absent and Muinremur accepted the challenge. "The rules are these," cried the giant, "you cut my head off tonight and I cut off yours tomorrow."

"Fair enough!" laughed Muinremur, who had no intention of keeping his side of the bargain with the foolish ogre. The ogre laid his head on the chopping block and Muinremur sliced off his head with an axe. To the surprise of them all, the ogre arose, took his head and walked off, saying that he would be back the next day. The following evening he returned but Muinremur was nowhere to be seen. The ogre protested at the outrage, and another warrior agreed to make the same bargain. On the following night that warrior also kept out of the way of the ogre. This happened for three nights and on the fourth night many people gathered in the court to witness the marvel. CuChulainn was present and the ogre challenged him to the game of beheading. CuChulainn not only knocked his head off with one blow but he also smashed it to bits on the floor. Even so the ogre arose, picked up the pieces and left. The following evening the ogre returned, knowing that CuChulainn was a hero who kept his word. "Where is the hero CuChulainn?" asked the ogre.

"I shall not hide from the likes of you," answered CuChulainn.

"You sound worried," said the ogre, "but at least you have kept your word." CuChulainn laid his neck on the block and the ogre raised his axe; everybody gasped and turned away. As he brought the axe down, the ogre turned the blade so that only the haft caught CuChulainn on the neck.

"Now rise up, CuChulainn!" cried the ogre, "for of all the heroes in Ulster and indeed in the whole of Ireland, you are the greatest in terms of valor and honor. You are champion of champions and the prize of Bricriu is for you alone. Your wife Emer is the first lady of Ulster. And if any of you dispute this fact, your days will be numbered." With these words the ogre left the room, but as he left he was transformed into Cu Roi, son of Daire, and

thus ensured that his judgment of the three heroes was to be final.

### THE MABINOGION

The story of Pwyll, Prince of Dyfed, who later receives the higher title of Chief of Annwn (the Underworld) for slaying the enemy of the King of the Underworld, is the first of the four "branches" of the Welsh *Mabinogion* collection. The tale reproduced below deals with the birth and childhood of Pwyll's son, Pryderi. This relatively late, written version has lost little of its early pagan quality. We are immediately plunged into a world where reality and myth intermingle: Human characters with earthly passions encounter Otherworld and Underworld characters; one moment we are in a recognizable Welsh landscape, the next we are in a magical country. The mythological themes in the *Mabinogion* include the fathering of an earthly hero by a god; the false slandering of the hero's mother; and the linking of the hero's birth with that of a colt, one of the most important animals for Celts. The story is punctuated by hunting, banqueting and lovemaking, reflecting the preoccupations of the early Celtic chieftains for whom these tales were composed.

**The birth of Pryderi –** Pwyll was at his court at Arbethy enjoying a great feast. After the first course, he felt like walking to the top of the mound, called Gorsedd Arberth, which towered up behind the court buildings. One of his courtiers warned him, "It is said that if a man of noble birth takes his seat on top of the mound of Gorsedd Arberth, he will either come away covered with wounds, or else he will have seen something wonderful."

"No one can harm me when I have so many of my men around me," Pwyll replied, "but

*Above: "The Death of CuChulainn" (bronze sculpture by Oliver Sheppard, The General Post Office, Dublin, Ireland). The Irish hero was mortally wounded by a spear thrown by his enemy Lugaid. In his desire to die upright and fighting he lashed himself to a stone pillar. Lugaid only dared to approach when the crow settled on CuChulainn's shoulder, signifying death.*

I should like to see this wonderful thing."

Pwyll and his men climbed the mound of Gorsedd Arberth, sat down, and waited. A lady appeared on the road beneath the mound. She rode a large pearly white steed, and was draped in silk brocaded with gold. The horse strode solemnly past the mound and Pwyll addressed his men: "Do any of you recognize the rider?" None of them answered. "Then one of you must go and ask her who she is." One of the men ran down the mound, but at the roadside she had disappeared. He set off after her, but the faster he ran the greater the distance between them. He gave up and returned to Pwyll: "Lord Chief of Annwn," said the man, "it is pointless to follow her on foot. "Then," replied Pwyll, "take the swiftest horse from the stables and catch her up."

The man galloped away but though his horse was fast and he used his spurs and whip, the lady receded from his view as before. The man returned to Pwyll: "Lord," he said, "there is no faster horse in Dyfed. We waste our time in following after her. "Yes," replied Pwyll, "magic is the only explanation."

On the following day they held another feast. After the first course Pwyll once again decided on a walk to the top of Gorsedd Arberth. A swift horse was taken with them. They had just taken their seats on the mound when the lady appeared once more, wearing the same dress and riding the same horse. "Look there," cried Pwyll, "Yesterday's rider. Now one of you, take the horse and go after her!" The lady was just at the foot of the mound riding, as before, at a solemn pace; one of the men started off after her at moderate canter. But still he could not catch her up, even though he broke into a gallop. Indeed the harder he drove his horse, the further she was from him. He gave up the chase and returned to Pwyll

at the mound. "Lord," he said, "you saw how hard I rode." "I saw," answered Pwyll, "there is no point in trying to catch her. But by the gods, there is some reason for her journey here, if only we could break her resolve to avoid us. Let us all return to the court."

That night was spend in drinking and singing. On the following day after dinner Pwyll said, "Everyone who was on the mound with me yesterday is to accompany me there once more." And he told his stable-groom to saddle his horse and bring his spurs. Up Gorsedd Arberth they went and they sat down. The lady came into view, in the same silken gold dress and on the same pearly white horse. After her rode Pwyll, but the faster he galloped the further she was from him. Soon he was riding as fast as he had ever ridden in his life, but he saw that he followed her in vain. So he called after her: "Lady, for the sake of the man you most love, wait for me."

"I am glad to do so," she replied, "and my horse wishes that you had made the request long ago." She waited for Pwyll and, drawing aside her head-dress, fixed him with her eyes and spoke with him.

"Lady," asked Pwyll, "where are you coming from and going to?"

"I go my own way," she answered, "and I am pleased to meet you." Pwyll thought that he had never seen a lady or maiden fairer than the one who was before him.

"Lady," he asked, "I would gladly know what you are doing in these parts."

"Then I shall tell you," she said, "it is you I come to see. My name is Rhiannon daughter of Hefeydd the Elder, and he has pledged me in marriage to a man I despise. For my part I will marry no man save yourself. This is the reason for my journey here." "My answer to you, by the gods," said Pwyll, "is that

*Below: The 'Monster of Noves' Bouches-du-Rhône, France. (c. fourth century BC.) Monsters devouring human bodies symbolised the triumph of death and the underworld over Earth's living creatures.*

there is no maiden or lady in the world that I would rather marry." "Then let us make a tryst," she said. "A year from now at the court of my father Hefeydd a feast shall be prepared for you." "I shall be there," said Pwyll. They went their separate ways and Pwyll changed the subject whenever his men questioned him about her.

A year later Pwyll set off with a hundred men. They rode to Hefeydd's court and were given a great welcome. At dinner Pwyll sat at the top of the table, with Rhiannon and her father on either side of him. They had finished the meat and were beginning their drinking-songs, when a striking young man with reddish-blond hair entered the hall. "The gods welcome to you," called out Pwyll to the man, for he looked of royal blood. "Please be seated." "I shall not," replied the man, "unless you grant me what I am here for." "You shall have what you desire," said Pwyll. "Why did you give such an answer?" cried Rhiannon too late. "He must keep his word," said the stranger, "in the presence of such nobles." "What is it you want, friend?" asked Pwyll. "You are feasting," he replied "and shall sleep tonight with the lady I most love, and I am here to take your place."

Pwyll was struck dumb by the stranger's words, and Rhiannon upbraided him for his stupidity: "This is Gwawl son of Clud, the man who wishes to marry me against my will, and now you must let him have me or you will be dishonored." Pwyll did not know what to say. "You must let him have me," continued Rhiannon, "and I shall make sure that he does not have me."

"How can that be?" asked Pwyll in bewilderment. "You can remain for the night's feasting, and I shall make a tryst with Gwawl: I shall promise to sleep with him in a year's

time, but you are to come to the trysting place with a hundred knights. Leave them in the orchard by the court. Enter the hall in rags and ask him to fill this small bag with food: I shall put a spell on it so that it can never be filled up. When he asks whether it will ever be full, you must answer: 'Only if the greatest in the kingdom presses the food in with his feet.' And when he has his feet in the bag you are to pull it over his head and tie it; then you must blow your hunting-horn as a signal for your hundred riders to take the court."

"Lord," interrupted Gwawl, "I am waiting for your answer." "You may take what is in my power to give," said Pwyll. "But these men of Dyfed," added Rhiannon, "are here as my guests, and they will enjoy the night's feasting. In one year's time I shall prepare a feast for you, and you shall sleep with me." Each chieftain returned to his own court.

*Above: Din Lligwy settlement, Anglesey, Wales. The entrance (right) of this late Iron-Age (fourth century AD) circular hut faces the central courtyard of a small Celtic settlement. It consisted of two circular and seven rectangular dwellings surrounded by a limestone wall; two of these contained evidence of iron smelting in their hearths. The roofs would have been of thatch.*

When the year was up Gwawl son of Clud came for his feast at Hefeydd's court. Pwyll Chief of Annwn also came, dressed in beggar's clothing as Rhiannon had told him. At the height of the merrymaking, he entered the hall. "May the gods be good to you and make you prosper," called out Gwawl. "The same to you sire," replied Pwyll, "and I should like to make a request." "So long as it is reasonable," said Gwawl, "you shall have what you ask." "Will you fill this small bag with food for me to keep the wolves from my door?" "A humble request," said he, and he called for the servants to fill the bag to the brim. They could not fill it and Gwawl asked: "Will the bag ever be full?" "Only," said Pwyll, "if the greatest man in the kingdom presses the food in with his feet." "Go on then, my man of valor," said Rhiannon to Gwawl. And Gwawl had no sooner stepped into the bag than it was up over his head and its thongs were knotted. Pwyll shed his rags and blew his horn. The hundred knights who

had hidden in the orchard were soon in the court; as each man entered the hall he smacked the bag and asked "What have we here?" "A badger," the others cried.

Inside the bag Gwawl protested: "This is no honorable death for me, to be battered to death in a bag." "He is right," added Hefeydd the Elder. "I accept what you say," said Pwyll, "but what must I do with him?" "This is what you must do," said Rhiannon. "The court poets and suitors are now at your command if Gwawl will make them over to you; and you must make him swear that he will not seek revenge for this night's events." "I swear," called Gwawl, and he was let out of the bag. "Rhiannon has laid down the terms," said Pwyll, "and you must keep them." "All I want," said Gwawl, "is to go home and take a bath for my bruises; my warriors can stay here as hostages." And Gwawl limped away. The night was spent in food and drink, each seated as he had sat a year earlier. Later, Rhiannon and Pwyll went to their bed and enjoyed one an-

other.

The next day Pwyll gave a feast for the court poets and suitors and all were content. At the end of the meal Pwyll addressed old Hefeydd: "Lord, with your permission I should like to return to Dyfed tomorrow." "That is allowed," said Hefeydd, "but give Rhiannon good notice of when you would like her to follow you." "Lord," answered Pwyll, "I should like her to accompany me." "Is that so?" asked Hefeydd. "Yes, by the gods," said Pwyll, "that is the way I shall have it."

In the morning they set out for the court of Arberth in Dyfed. A warm welcome awaited them. A feast was prepared and all the most important lords and ladies in the kingdom were present. Pwyll sent each one off with a gift to remember him by: some took brooches, some rings, and some took jewels. Pwyll and Rhiannon brought prosperity to Dyfed over the next two years.

In the third year of their reign, the leading men of Dyfed summoned Pwyll to a place

*Right: Bronze fittings on a wooden bucket from Aylewsford Kent, England. The helmeted head on the handle mount suggests that the bucket was used in a warrior ritual.*

called Preseleu and counseled him to take another wife, since Rhiannon had not produced a child. Pwyll persuaded them to be patient for one more year.

Before the year was out, a baby was born to Rhiannon and Pwyll at the court of Arberth. Six women were called in to watch the boy's first night with Rhiannon; but by midnight they were all asleep, and when the cock crew they awoke to find the baby gone. "What are we to do?" the women cried, "for Rhiannon will blame us." One of them answered: "Look here, there is a hound in the corner with pups; let us kill the pups and scatter their bones in Rhiannon's lap and smear her with the blood; all six of us will swear that she has killed her own baby."

As the sun rose Rhiannon woke up and asked for her son. "Lady," replied the women, "we tried to stop you, but see, you have battered your baby to death in the middle of the night." "You know that you are making this up," answered Rhiannon, "but I shall not harm you if you tell me the truth." But the women kept to their story, and although Pwyll trusted Rhiannon's word, the druids gave her a punishment: She was to sit outside the court by the horse-mounting block for seven years, and offer to carry in any man who would let her. Few allowed her to do this, but in this manner she spent most of that year.

In those days Teyrnon Twryf Liant ruled Gwent Is-Coed. He was the finest of men. He owned a mare more beautiful than any in the kingdom. Every year on the eve of May, the mare would foal, but no one had ever seen her colt. "This May-Eve," said Teyrnon to his wife, "I shall sit up and watch and find out who or what is taking our colts." He had the mare brought into his room and in the middle of the night a colt was born: It was a hand-

some colt, large and already standing where it was born. Teyrnon was just remarking what a fine colt it was when there was a sudden crash: A giant claw came through the window and grabbed the colt's mane. In a flash Teyrnon had drawn his sword and lopped off the monstrous arm at the elbow. There was a great scream from the courtyard and Teyrnon rushed out but could see nothing in the darkness. Remembering that he had left the door open behind him he gave up the pursuit and ran back to his room. In the doorway was a baby boy in swaddling-clothes, wrapped in a gold brocaded silk sheet.

Teyrnon took the boy into his wife's room. "My lady," he called, "are you asleep?" And Teyrnon told her what had happened in the

*Above: "Rhiannon" (watercolor by Alan Lee; 1981). Alan Lee's illustrations for the* Mabinogion *combine Celtic decorative features with Romantic medievalist images. Here, Rhiannon appears as a medieval Arthurian princess looking back at her pursuers. Her birds were harbingers of the Otherworld and their singing at Harlech in the tale of Branwen suspends earthly time.*

night and that he had a noble son for her. "I shall pretend that he is our own child, since we have never had one," she said. The boy was taken to the holy stone and baptized by a druid. He was named Gwri of the Golden Hair, for his head was ablaze with gold. By the end of the year Gwri was already walking confidently about the court like a three-year-old. After two years he was more like a boy of six. And before he was four he was already arguing with the stable-hands to let him take their horses to water. Teyrnon's wife recalled the handsome colt that was born on the night the boy appeared and she had it broken in for Gwri to ride.

In the meantime they heard the news concerning Rhiannon and her punishment. Teyrnon Twryf Liant wondered at the story, for it had happened on the same May-Eve that the boy had been found. Teyrnon had often been amazed at the striking resemblance between the foundling and Pwyll Chief of Annwn, and he now realized the truth. His wife agreed that their Gwri of the Golden Hair should be sent to Rhiannon: "We shall gain three things by doing this," she said. "Rhiannon's gratitude for releasing her from her punishment; Pwyll's favor for looking after their boy and educating him; and, moreover, should the boy grow into a hero, he shall be our foster-son and do good deeds for us."

The following day saw Teyrnon and two of his knights riding toward Arberth. Gwri rode beside them on the handsome colt. As they approached the court a woman called to them from the horse-mounting block: "Let me take you both the rest of your journey on my back, for I killed my son in my sleep with my own hands." "None of us will go on your back," said Teyrnon, "but we shall walk beside you."

The hall was filled with sounds of rejoicing at the homecoming of Rhiannon's son. Pwyll and Rhiannon placed Teyrnon between them at table; on the other side of Pwyll sat Teyrnon's two knights with the boy between them. After dinner the drinking began and each told their own wonderful tale. Teyrnon told of the mare and the foundling boy, and everyone present saw the features of Pwyll in the boy's countenance.

"If this really is my own son," cried Rhiannon, "I shall be delivered of my care." "This phrase of yours shall be his name," said Pendaran of Dyfed, "Pryderi, for that means 'Care' in our Celtic speech!" "Though Gwri of the Golden Hair is also a fitting name," said Pwyll, "it is most fitting that he has the name his mother cried when she heard that he was safe; Pryderi, son of Pwyll Chief of Annwn." Teyrnon Twryf Liant and his wife were praised by the assembly and Pwyll and Rhiannon offered them gifts of fine horses, hounds, and jewels; but Teyrnon Twryf Liant refused them all and went back home content with the praise.

Pwyll and Rhiannon placed Pryderi in the care of the noble Pendaran of Dyfed. Pwyll grew old and died and Pryderi grew into a handsome hero and was loved by the people of the seven cantrefs of Dyfed. His conquests took in the three cantrefs of Ystrad Tywi and the four of Ceredigiawn: these are the seven cantrefs of Seisyllwch. And one day Pryderi son of Pwyll Chief of Annwn married Cifga, daughter of Gwyn Gohoyw, son of Gloyw Wallt Lydan, son of Casnar Wledig: these were the sons of the high kings of this island.

Here ends the first branch of the *Mabinogion*.

*Left: "Olwen" (watercolor by Alan Lee; 1981). Olwen, another character from the* Mabinogion *collection, is depicted in the midst of nature, associated with the Celtic Otherworld. The side frames show the warriors of Arthur's court banqueting as they discuss Culhwch's request for the hand of the unknown Olwen.*

# CELTIC GODS AND GODDESSES

We know from various references in myths and legends, and from religious inscriptions of the Roman period in Gaul and Britain, that the Celts worshipped a bewildering array of magical gods and goddesses. However, although we may know the names of many Celtic deities, their natures and mythical "biographies" remain elusive compared to the surviving divine stories of other ancient cultures. One reason for this is that Celtic artists rarely produced anthromorphic (humanlike) images before they came under Greek influence in the La Tène period. Therefore the relatively late representations of Celtic divinities, produced by artists trained in the Graeco-Roman style, are not very helpful in telling us about original Celtic perceptions of their gods. Likewise, we must be careful about relying too much on the evidence of classical authors, or on the later versions of Celtic myths written down by Christians, because these writers might have adapted or omitted any blatant pagan elements in the original sources.

The principal source of evidence about the gods of the insular Celts comes from myths such as the Ulster cycle and the Mabinogion. Another important source of information on the Irish Celts' deities is the pseudo-history The Book of Invasions, a twelfth-century version of the mythical explanation of the Irish people's origins. It tells the story of a number of invasions of Ireland, one of which was by the Tuatha de Danaan, "The People of the Goddess Danu." According to the legend, these magical figures were the original Irish gods.

Upon their arrival in Ireland the Tuatha de Danaan demanded battle or the kingship from the Fir Bholg, who at the time ruled the land. The First Battle of the Magh Tuiredh then followed, during which the Fir Bholg were

*Left: Human and animal warriors (bronze matrix for making helmet plaques; from Torslunda, Sweden; eighth century AD). Teutonic warriors of pre-Viking Sweden, like their Celtic neighbors, decorated their helmets. Shape-shifting from human into animal form is a regular feature of Celtic mythology, particularly among the gods.*

defeated. Soon after this the Tuatha de Danaan had to do battle again, this time against a race of demonic beings called the Fomhoire. The battle, known as the Second Battle of the Magh Tuiredh, was a great slaughter on both sides, but ended up with the Tuatha de Danaan routing the Fomhoire, who were expelled for ever from Ireland. Before long, however, the Tuatha de Danaan themselves were defeated and confined for eternity to the Otherworld by the Sons of Míl, who had come to Ireland from Spain, and whose descendants, the Gaels, were henceforth to be the dominant people of Ireland.

The father-figure of the Tuatha de Danaan was Daghdha, literally "Good God." He was said to have been very wise, and another of his names describes him as the Ruadh Rofhessa, "The Mighty One of Great Knowledge." He possessed the skills of sorcery and was consequently also the god of druidism. He had two special attributes, his club and his cauldron. With one end of his club he killed the living, while with the other he revived the dead. When he dragged it behind him it left deep tracks in the ground. The cauldron was a traditional symbol of the Celtic Otherworld, a vessel "from which no company ever went unsatisfied." Its possession identified Daghdha as a lord of the Otherworld, and gave him his reputed ability "to control the weather and the crops."

Our knowledge of the Gaulish gods comes principally from the written account of Julius Caesar. He wrote "Of all the gods, they worship Mercury most of all. He has the greatest number of images; they hold that he is the inventor of all the arts and a guide on the roads and on journeys, and they believe him the most influential for money-making and commerce. After him they honor Apollo, Mars, Jupiter and Minerva. Of these deities they have almost the same idea as other peoples: Apollo drives away diseases, Minerva teaches the first principles of the arts and crafts, Jupiter rules the heavens and Mars controls the issues of war."

We must treat Caesar's words with a certain degree of suspicion. Not only does he imply the existence of a pantheon of gods who were worshiped more or less universally throughout the whole of Gaul, but also he suggests that the Gauls' conception of the gods differed little from that of other peoples, with each one having a clearly defined divine function. It seems that Caesar has reduced the abundance and variety of the Gaulish divinity to a convenient and manageable schema comprehensible to his fellow Romans. Archeological and documented evidence have shown that in reality the names and types of gods worshiped varied greatly from tribe to tribe, and from region to region. There are numerous references in Celtic mythology to local gods and cults of a particular tribe, for example. Similarly, there is little evidence to prove that there was such a neat separation of divine functions as described by Caesar. Apart from a few exceptions, for example those deities who had clearly

*Above: Cocidius as Silvanus, the Roman hunter deity (jasper seal-stone from near Northumberland, England; second to fourth centuries AD). Cocidius was a native Celtic hunter god, whose worship was taken up by Roman soldiers defending northern England.*

*Above: Dedicatory inscription to Mars (Allones, France; late first century AD). After the Roman conquest of Gaul, native Celtic deities continued to be worshiped and were often combined with the imperial gods. Mars Mullo was a Romano-Celtic mule god who was incorporated with the Roman war god, Mars. At Allones he was worshiped as a healer of eye disease.*

*Right: Head of the Romano-British deity Antenociticus (c. third century AD). This local Celtic god was worshiped in a small temple near a Roman military fort on Hadrian's wall. The head is carved in the classical manner, but its Celtic features shine through in the powerfully modeled hair and eyes.*

defined specific roles, such as the Irish Dian Cécht the leech and Giobhniu the smith, most gods had a range of functions and were not assigned to any particular sphere of human activity as were the classical gods. The result is a confusing but fascinating tangle of gods, goddesses and cults.

### THE CELTIC GODS
### GAULISH "MERCURY": IRISH LUGH

Many Celtic deities, as well as sacred rituals, became intermingled with their Graeco-Roman counterparts during the period of Roman domination. Not only did many Romans adopt elements of the Celtic religion, but also the Celts followed a number of Roman religious practices. For example, Mercury, the god of merchants and inventor of all the arts, found his Celtic equivalent in Lugh, who in Irish mythology is also called *ildánach*, "skilled in all the arts." According to Caesar, Mercury was the most honored of all the Gaulish gods. Several images of him closely resemble those of the classical Mercury: They show him as a beardless youth, wearing a winged hat and carrying a purse and a herald's wand; usually he is accompanied by a cock, ram, or tortoise. Sometimes, however, he is shown bearded and wearing Gaulish dress. He is often associated with the goddess Maia, who represents wealth and abundance. Unlike the classical Mercury, the Gaulish god's arts included war.

In Ireland, we learn from *The Book of Invasions* that Lugh, whose name means "The Shining One," was the most colorful figure of the Tuatha de Danaan. He appears as youthful, athletic, and handsome, and a victor over malevolent Otherworld beings. He is also described as the divine father of CuChulainn, the brave warrior from the Ulster cycle of

myths. In the tale of the Second Battle of Magh Tuiredh it is explained that Lugh commanded all the arts possessed by the many craftsmen in the house of King Nuadha. Lugh came to the royal court during a great feast. The doorkeeper asked what skill he possessed, since no one without a special skill could enter. "I am a wright," said Lugh. "We do not require you; we have a wright already." "I am a smith," said Lugh, but the doorkeeper replied that they had one of those too. Lugh continued to list his various skills – champion, hero, poet, sorcerer, cupbearer, craftsman – but each time the doorkeeper replied that the Tuatha de Danaan had experts in each field. Lugh then asked if anyone combined all these skills. Naturally they did not and Lugh was allowed to enter.

Lugh possessed a magical spear, which ensured victory whenever it was used. However, during the Second Battle of Magh

Tuiredh, the most important battle in Irish mythology, Lugh used a sling-shot to kill his dreaded adversary, Balar of the baleful eye. According the legend, Nuadha had stepped down as king to allow Lugh defend Ireland against the Fomhoire. Lugh was said to have been the "divine prototype of human kingship," attended by a young and regally dressed woman, who can be identified as the sovereignty of Ireland.

The cult of Lugh was not confined to the Irish Celts. In Wales he was known as Lleu, and appears in the tale of Math vab Mathonwy as a shoemaker. An inscription found at Osma in Spain bears a dedication to the Lugoves (the plural of Lugus, the older form of Lugh's name) on behalf of a guild of shoemakers. A similar inscription appears in Avenches, Switzerland. Lugh's name also make an appearance in the place-name Lugudunon, Latin Lugudunum, from which derive the modern names Lyon and Laon in France, Leiden in Holland, and Leignitz in Silesia. Similarly, the Roman name for Carlisle in the north of England, Luguvalium, derives from Luguvalos meaning "He who is strong like Lugus." These widespread references to Lugh suggest that he was known and worshiped throughout the Celtic world.

### GAULISH "APOLLO"

Like many classical writers, Caesar equates the Gaulish god "who drives away diseases" with the Roman god Apollo. In particular, he is the god of healing thermal springs. There are numerous inscriptions dedicated to this divinity and it is clear that "Apollo" enjoyed an extensive and popular cult. However, the dedications use a number of different names to identify the god, several of which occur relatively frequently and seem to refer to

separate deities. The most common of these – Belenus – can be found in inscriptions in the old Celtic kingdom of Noricum in the eastern Alps, northern Italy, southern Gaul, and Britain. The ancient Irish feast May-Eve, or Beltene, which means "brilliant, shining fire," probably derives from his name. This, together with the fact that he is equated with the Roman Apollo, suggest that Belenus was associated with the sun. Another of the names for "Apollo" was Grannus. According to legend, he was credited with healing powers and was invoked by the emperor Caracalla in AD 215. His female companion is usually identified as the goddess Sirona, whose title comes from the word for "star." Borvo is the Gaulish name most associated with thermal waters. His name signifies boiling water and is preserved in place-names such as Bourbonne-les-Bains.

Another Gaulish name associated with the god of healing springs is Maponos. Worship of this deity was not restricted to Gaul, but

*Below: The Gundestrup Cauldron, Denmark (first century BC). This interior silver panel represents a divinity and warrior grappling with a wheel. The god could be any one of a number of Celtic sky divinities. The wheel is a solar symbol in Celtic art, and the griffins that appear across the bottom of the panel were traditionally associated with Apollo.*

*Below: Gaulish stone with Celtic inscription (Vieux-Poitiers, France; c. first century* AD*). Our knowledge of the ancient Celtic language comes from place-names, names of tribes and kings on coins, and inscriptions carved on altars or sacred stones. The letter-forms were borrowed mainly from the Latin of contemporary Romans; Greek letters were sometimes used in southern Gaul.*

was common elsewhere in the Celtic world, particularly in the north of England. There he was also credited with the art of music and was known as a hunter. Maponos appears in Welsh literature as Mabon son of Modron, "The Divine Mother," the eponymous goddess of the Marne River in France. He also survives in continental Arthurian romance as Mabon, as well as Mabuz and Mabonagrain.

In Ireland the closest parallel to Mabon-Maponos is Mac ind Óg, "The Young Lad," who was the son of Daghdha, chief god of the Irish, and Boann, wife of the water deity Nechtan and eponym of the great river of Irish mythology. However, although Mac ind Óg is thus associated with water, just like the Gaulish "Apollo," he is not normally connected with healing. This is the role of Dian Cécht, one of the craft-gods of the Tuatha de Danaan. In the Second Battle of Magh Tuiredh, for example, he brings the dead of the Tuatha de Danaan back to life, ensuring his people's victory against the Fomhoire. It is clear from this that the insular Celtic gods Mabon, Mac ind Óg, and Dian Cécht embody only certain aspects of the Gaulish figures traditionally grouped under the title "Apollo."

### GAULISH OGMIOS: IRISH OGHMA

According to the Roman writer Lucian, who wrote in the second century AD, the Celts worshiped Hercules under the name Ogmios. Lucian describes a Gaulish image of this god, armed with club and bow normally attributed to the Roman god, but uncharacteristically old, bald, and gray, with skin darkened and wrinkled by the sun. A group of men are attached to him by thin chains that link their ears to the tip of his tongue, which reflects the Celtic association of Ogmios with eloquence. Although little is known for certain about

Ogmios, most scholars agree that he can be identified with Oghma, a figure from Irish mythology. Like Ogmios, Oghma's main attribute is his strength: He is also known as a *trénfher*, literally a "strong man" or "divine champion."

### GAULISH "DIS PATER": IRISH DONN

Caesar records how the Gaulish Celts were taught by their druids that they were all descended from Dis Pater, the Roman god of the dead. This concept of common descent was an essential belief of Celts everywhere. Different Irish tribes, for example, traced their genealogies to various divine ancestors. Dieties such as Lugh were the reputed founders of many scattered peoples. Daghdha, the chief god of the Tuatha de Danaan, was sometimes called "The Great Father," while Nuadha, another of the Tuatha de Danaan kings, was said to be the progenitor of all the Irish. However, Donn, another Irish god revered as an ancestor deity, can be more closely identified with Dis Pater in that he, too, was a god of the dead. According to Irish mythology, Donn's abode is a small rocky island, now known as Tech Duinn, "The House of Donn," off the southwest coast of Ireland. He invites his descendants, the people of Ireland, to come to house when they die. Donn, "the brown, or dark, one," often represents the somber aspect of the Underworld, and is even sometimes assimilated with the Devil. However, he is a complex god who is both benign and terrible, creator of storms and shipwrecks, but protector of cattle and crops.

### MANANNÁN MAC LIR

It is perhaps not surprising that the Irish, whose homeland was completely surrounded by water should have known a god of the sea. In fact

they may have had several, but the only one to be documented is Manannán mac Lir, literally "son of the sea." His traditional home is the Isle of Man, and the waters with which he best identified are those between the northeast coast of Ireland and the northwest of Britain. He was also associated with the supernatural island of Emhain Ablach, which has been identified as the Isle of Arran in the Firth of Clyde. In *The Book of Invasions* he is not mentioned as a member of the Tuatha de Danaan, but in later texts he is included in their number. In one story he leads King Cormac mac Airt to his Otherworld court. He

*Above: Gold boat model (from Broighter, County Derry, Ireland; first century BC). This miniature boat, complete with benches, mast, and oars, was part of a hoard of gold jewelry and may have been an offering to a water deity, such as the Irish sea god Manannán mac Lir.*

*Above: The horned god Cernunnos (Romano-Celtic relief sculpture, Paris, France; first century AD). The god of wild beasts, the most represented of all Celtic gods, is shown here in human form with the ears and antlers of a stag: from each antler hangs a torc, symbol of the Celtic warrior class. Cernunnos was popular in Gaul, but there are very few references to him in Irish and British art and mythology, although he appears later as the antler-horned Herne the Hunter.*

from around the fourth century BC. It shows a deity with antlers, human as well as a deer's ears, and wearing torcs – jewelry worn by Celtic warriors – and accompanied by a horned serpent. The carving records the name of the god as "[C]ernunnos, the Horned (or Peaked) One," which now refers to all similar images. On the Gundestrup cauldron, Cernunnos appears as "Lord of the Animals." He holds a ram-headed serpent in his left hand, and on his right stands a magnificent stag. Various other animals are scattered around. Archeological evidence has shown that the horned god was familiar to the Celts of Scotland and Ireland, too. The name of Conall Cernach, one of CuChulainn's rivals in the Ulster cycle of myths, may have derived from the deity's title. Both hunter and protector of animals, Cernunnos has persisted in British folk tradition as Herne the Hunter.

## CELTIC GODDESSES
### GAULISH MINERVA: IRISH BRIGHID
Caesar included the Roman goddess Minerva among the major deities of Gaul. In fact a number of the mother-goddesses that are so fundamental to Celtic mythology can be assimilated to her. It is not clear whether Caesar was referring to all of these goddesses or just a single representative, but what is evident is that his description of "Minerva" as a patron of the arts and crafts does not give a full enough picture of the complex and far-reaching functions of the female deities nor their all-pervasive influence on the Celtic peoples. As the patron of arts and crafts "Minerva" is represented on a number of carvings together Mercury and Vulcan, a grouping that emphasizes the great importance of technical skills in Celtic society. As patron of the art of healing she was honored at thermal

is described as "the rider of the crested sea," the waves are his steed and when the sea is agitated "the tresses of Manannán's wife are tossed." It is thought that Manannán mac Lir had a close, although not an exact, counterpart in the British god Manawydan fab Llyr.

All Celtic mythology abounds with images of gods associated with animals or birds. In some sculptures they are shown accompanied by creatures, while in others the gods themselves take animal forms. In some cases, however, the gods simply have certain animal features. The most notable of these is the "horned god," who may bear the horns of a stag, ram, or bull. The earliest Celtic representation of such a god is a stone carving found at Val Camonica in northern Italy, and dates springs, such as those at Bath in southern England, where she was was identified with the goddess Sulis.

In Ireland Minerva's nearest counterpart was Brighid, who was apparently expert in poetry, learning, and prophecy, and was worshipped by the *filidh*. Brighid was the daughter of Daghdha and had two sisters, both also named Brighid, one associated with healing, the other with craftsmanship. Like a number of Celtic goddesses, she has given her name to rivers: the Brighid in Ireland, the Braint in Wales, the Brent in England. Such was her prestige in Ireland that the name Brighid became synonymous with the word "goddess." Her cult was so established that it continued virtually uninterrupted when Christianity came to the country: the early Christians merely transformed her into St. Brigit, or Bride, and declared her to be the founder of the first Irish nunnery.

## OTHER GODDESSES

Unlike the Greeks and Romans, the Celts had no goddess of love. Even so, the female divinities display vigorous sexuality. For example, the legendary Queen Medb of Connaught, who features in the Ulster cycle of Irish mythology, had an insatiable sexual appetite and claimed that "never was she without one man in the shadow of another." This particular characteristic of Celtic goddesses is bound up with their function as divine mother and their identification with the land. In their literature, all the Celts, especially the Irish Celts, show a concern with the land on which live. Every physical feature has its own name, and each has its own particular legend, in which female divinities play the principal role. In Gaul the earth-goddesses were collectively honored under the

title of Matres, or Matronae, but this tradition can be found in all Celtic areas. In Ireland the divine people, the Tuatha de Danaan, are reputed to have been born of the goddess Danu. Likewise, the Welsh Celts all claimed to have issued from Dôn, and Wales, like Gaul, had its "Great Mother" Modron. To these should be added the numerous goddesses who were associated with and gave their name to certain localities – a province, a mountain, a river.

An important aspect of insular Celtic mythology is that in most instances the rulers of the supernatural realm are goddesses not gods. Similarly, in early Irish tales the Otherworld is described as "The Land of Women." This

*Above: "St. Bride" (John Duncan, tempera on canvas; 1913). The pagan Celtic goddess Brighid was daughter of Daghdha, one of the original Irish gods, the Tuatha de Danaan. Around AD 450 she was transformed into the Christian St. Brigit, or Bride, founder of the first nunnery at Kildare. A Scottish legend tells us of her travelling from Iona to Bethlehem and returning with the baby Jesus. Duncan portrays her equally as the pagan bringer of Spring, being carried by angels across the Sound of Iona.*

*Right: Head of "Medusa the Gorgon"
(pediment of the Temple of Sulis Minerva,
Bath, England; first century* AD). *The Greek
female monster, with her snake-locks, was
often used as an apotropaic figure in Greek
and Roman religious contexts to "avert the
evil eye." Here "she" has become a "he"
complete with mustache and staring eyes in
the Celtic style. Medusa's head was worn
by Minerva on her breastplate to
petrify her enemies; her worship was
combined with that of Sulis, the Celtic
goddess of the healing waters of Bath.
However, this "Gorgon" has many unusual
features, which may signify a Celtic sun
deity, perhaps the consort of Sulis.*

confirms the notion that the insular Celts generally believed in a great goddess who was mother of all gods. On Celtic monuments these "mother-goddesses" usually appear in groups of three. They carry baskets of fruit, trays of loaves or cakes, cornucopias, babies, or other symbols of their connection with the land and fertility. In the myths, several of these goddesses appear as consorts of male deities, a mythological coupling that ensures not only the security of a tribe or nation but also its prosperity. Often the goddess assumes the dominant role in her marriage. Queen Medb, for example, was a formidable character who not only ruthlessly humiliated her submissive husbands, but also personally led the armies of Connaught against the Ulstermen.

Medb is not the only Irish goddess to display warlike characteristics. Several, including Buanann, "The Lasting One," "mother of heroes" and Scáthach, "The Shadowy One," taught martial arts to young warriors. Above all, however, a number can be described as goddesses of war. Although these occasionally appeared singly they are normally conceived in group of three. These comprise the Morríghan, "Phantom Queen" and the Badhbh, "Crow," or "Raven," accompanied by Nemhain, "Frenzy" or by Macha, who gave her name to Emuin Machae, capital of the ancient province of Ulster and seat of Conchobar, and to Ard Macha, modern Armagh. Normally these war-goddesses do not take part in the fighting themselves: They simply use magic and their terrifying presence as their weapons. The very appearance of Medb, for instance, deprived the enemy two-thirds of their strength, while Nemhain, as her name suggests, creates panic among fighting men; when she raised her cry over the armies facing CuChulainn "a hundred

warriors of them fell dead that night of terror and fright."

War-goddesses were also known elsewhere in the Celtic world. The Cathubodua, "crow, raven of battle" of the Haute-Savoie corresponds

*Below: The goddess Epona on horseback. This Celtic deity was the patroness of horses. She may be linked with Rhiannon in the story of Pwyll. In her right hand she holds a rose-garland, offered to her by worshipers.*

*Above: Bronze boar from Bata, Hungary (second century BC). The wild boar remained a symbol of the warrior's ferocity throughout the pagan Celtic period. This figurine may have been worn as a helmet crest. The raised dorsal bristles symbolize the animal's aggression: in the myths, the hair of Celtic warriors similarly stands on end when they go into battle.*

to Badhbh. In Wales, the name of the Aeron River is derived from the Celtic Agrona, "goddess of slaughter." Similarly, the Celts in England worshiped the goddess Andraste, whom Boudicca invoked before going into battle.

### CELTIC CULTS OF NATURE
As we have already seen, Celtic goddesses were related to particular physical features of the land, these divine mothers being perceived as personifications of the fruitful earth. However, there were several other Celtic cults of deities who represented or who were associated with the land. There were gods of the mountain, the field, the rock, and the fortified place. Rivers normally had their own gods, too: for example, the Seine (dea Sequana), the Saône (Souconna), and the many rivers whose names

simply mean "divine." Equally common was the cult of the sacred tree. In England and elsewhere druids have traditionally been associated with the oak. In Gaul inscriptions and names prove the existence of widespread tree-cults. The Irish Celts had a special term for the sacred tree, *bile*, which may be related to the Gaulish *Biliomagus*, "The Plain of the Sacred Tree." Throughout Celtic mythology are references to to great trees, the Oak of Mughna, the Yew of Ross, and the Ash of Uisneach being just three examples. It seems that each tribe had its own sacred tree, which stood on the site where the kings of the tribe were crowned, and which may have embodied the tribe's security. Often an invading force would chop down a tribe's sacred tree, a gesture designed to demoralize the enemy.

Many animals and birds also had special cult status for the Celts, and sacred or supernatural beasts frequently appear in their mythology. The horned god, Cernunnos, was associated with the stag, the ram-headed serpent, the bull, and indirectly the entire animal kingdom, while the Irish goddess Flidhais ruled over all the animals in the forests. Boars, horses, dogs, and bears, as well as various types of fish and birds, were all connected with certain gods. Perhaps the most important of these creatures was the boar, which is represented on numerous statues and carvings, and features in several myths. It is often a fierce, destructive animal that leads its hunters to the Otherworld. In the Welsh tale "Culhwch and Olwen," for example, Mabon pursues and catches a magic boar called Twrch Trwyth. In other cases gods and goddesses are shown sitting on the back of a wild boar, a sign of their power over nature. Celts considered pork the choicest of foods, the "champion's portion," and in Irish legend the

undiminishing food of the Otherworld is sometimes shown in the form of a pig, which though killed and eaten each evening, is alive again the following morning. Celtic warriors also had symbols of the boar as their helmet crests.

Supernatural horses, too, are important characters in Celtic mythology. Horse-riding was one of the pleasures especially associated with the Otherworld. Epona, "The Divine Horse" or "The Horse Goddess," was one of the most important of the Gaulish and English divinities, and was even worshiped by the Roman

*Below: Bull-headed terminal of iron fire-dog, Capel Garmon, Denbigh, Wales (c. first century BC). One of a pair used to support roasting spits over a fire, the bull was a Celtic symbol of virility and would have been a fitting decoration at a warrior banquet.*

*Left: Warriors with boar-crested helmets (bronze matrix for making decorative helmet plaques, from Torslunda, Sweden; eighth century AD). Cultural links between pre-Viking Scandinavia and the Celts are reflected in similar warrior aristocracies wearing similar armor: such boar crests are found in a number of representations of Celtic warriors.*

*Below: Uffington White Horse, Oxfordshire, England (chalk-carved figure; c. first century BC to first century AD). This may represent the horse-goddess Epona, the patron deity of the local Dobunni Celts.*

cavalry during their period of occupation of Gaul and England. The Dobunni tribe of Celts from the south of England may have carved the massive chalk horse near Oxford in her honor. Epona may have corresponded to the Rhiannon, the mysterious horse-rider who appears in the Welsh *Mabinogion*, and she may also have a counterpart in the Irish goddess Edain Echraidhe.

Magic or sacred birds are equally common. While some deities occasionally assume the form of birds, others constantly do so. The warlike goddesses the Badhbh, for example, changed into ravens or hooded crows, a sign of impending death. Others, associated with the joyous Otherworld, lull men to sleep with their beautiful sweet voices. The image of swans linked by a silver chain – the symbol of metamorphosed gods – is a common motif in Celtic art.

*Left: "The Children of Lir" (bronze sculpture by Oisin Kelly, the Garden of Remembrance, Phoenix Park, Dublin; erected after the 1916 Easter Rising). This sculpture depicts the characters from one of the Irish Celtic* Three Sorrowful Tales of Erin, *the other two being* Deirdre of the Sorrows *and* The Children of Tuireann. *The sculptor has depicted the moment in the tale when the swan-children metamorphose from human to animal form, a common ability of the Celtic gods. Silver chains link the swan-children, a token of their fairy status.*

# CELTIC RELIGION AND RELIGIOUS PRACTICES

**O**ur understanding of Celtic religion is hindered, more than any other aspect of the Celtic world, by the lack of written sources, and the difficulties involved in interpreting archeological evidence. These problems are increased by the secret nature of many Celtic religious cults, which was in part due to the great political respect commanded by Celtic priests and their consequent elitism. Therefore, we have to turn to the limited observations of ancient non-Celtic authors, whose writings are often biased by their view of the Celts as primitive barbarians. But by using these classical secondary sources, together with archeological remains and the evidence presented within the myths themselves, we can partially reconstruct the mysterious religion of the Celts.

### DRUIDS AND PROPHETS

The Greek writer Diodorus of Sicily, writing his "mythical history" in the first century BC, tells us a great deal about the religious practices of the Gaulish Celts. In particular, he refers to the high social status and learning of the Celtic druids: "Those men called by us philosophers and theologians are held in great honor by them; they call them 'Druids' ... and no sacrifice may be performed without a Druid present ... for only they speak the language of the gods." The Celts not only believed that the druids had a special relationship with the gods, they also conceived the druids as being almost semidivine. In Ireland, for example, the Celts believed the druids were descended from Daghdha, the god of druidism and the father of all the Irish Tuatha de Danaan gods. This meant that the druids were favored by the deities, and therefore special and worthy of respect.

Although the druids were not worshiped themselves, they nonetheless dominated the spiritual life of their tribes. They led all religious ceremonies and rituals, prepared magic potions and libations in their cauldrons, recited incantations and curses, and invoked the power of the gods in time of need. The druidic control of religious affairs accounts for the many occasions in Celtic myths when they are consulted by clan-chiefs and kings – like Greek oracles, they were able to influence political and social decisions. Julius Caesar, too, refers to their great authority in Celtic society not only in religion but also in more material concerns, such as educational and legal affairs. It was the druids who had the responsibility of educat-

*Previous page: "The Druids: Bringing in the Mistletoe" (by George Henry and E A Hornel; 1890). The Roman writer, Pliny the Elder, relates that on the sixth day of the moon, the druids climbed a sacred oak and cut off the mistletoe with a golden sickle.*

*Right: The "Druid's Stone," Dartmoor, England. The hole in the rock was formed by the continuous action of running water. A local legend refers to the stone as a place of druid baptism: The initiate would be passed through the hole into the stream below.*

ing the tribe's young warrior nobles and passing judgment in disputes. Caesar adds that the druids' privileges included exemption from taxation and military service. That is not to say, however, that they did not contribute to the tribe's military campaigns in other ways instead. In the Irish mythological pseudohistory *The Book of Invasions*, for example, King Lugh of the Tuatha de Danaan calls on a druid to cast three showers of fire upon the enemy Fomhoire, to deprive them of two-thirds of their strength and valor, and to bind in their bodies the urine of horses and humans.

According to Caesar, students of the Gaulish druidic religion had to "learn many verses by heart, sometimes for a period of twenty years. It is considered sacrilege to put their teachings into writing." Celtic religion was thus intended to mysterious and exclusive. Caesar also says that one Gaulish druid

held chief authority over all the druids, and that they would all meet in assembly at a holy place in the lands of Carnutes, the legendary center of Gaul. Likewise, the Irish druids elected a leader and met at Uisneach, the "navel" of Ireland and reputedly the site of a great assembly. Similar parallels can be seen between the religions of the other Celtic peoples, too, and it seems that the druidic system was virtually universal in the Celtic world. Certainly Caesar tells us that the Gaulish system had originally been exported to Gaul from Britain. Archeological and documentary evidence suggests that druidic practices also occurred as far away as Galatia. The geographer Strabo tells us that the council of Galatian druids met in assembly at a place known as the "oak-sanctuary," one of many references to the tree traditionally associated with druids.

The importance of prophets in Celtic religion was also recorded by Diodorus: "These men predict the future by observing the flight and calls of the birds, and by the sacrifice of holy animals: All orders of society are in their power … and in very important matters they prepare a human victim, plunging a dagger into his chest; by observing the way his limbs convulse as he falls and the gushing of his blood, they are able to read the future." There are numerous incidents in Celtic mythology of prophets warning heroes of an impending tragedy, or else foretelling who was destined to be victorious. Prophets were also employed in selecting who was to be the next king. The selection process, known as *tarbhfhess*, meaning "bull-feast" or "bull-sleep," involved a bull being killed, the prophet eating his fill of its flesh and drinking its broth, before laying down to sleep. As the prophet slept,

*Below: The Gundestrup Cauldron, Denmark. (first century BC.) On this silver inner panel of the guil-silver ritual vessel, the artist depicted warriors going into battle, preceded by a ram-horned snake.*

*Right: Dragon Hill, Uffington, England. This hill is rich in Celtic legends. One tells of St. George killing the dragon on the summit: No grass can grow where its blood was spilled, hence the bare chalky patch.*

honor of "the fire of Bel" (an ancient god of life and death), domestic fires were extinguished and rekindled from a new druidic fire. Winter began on the first of November, preceded by the feast of Samhain (our Halloween), which also marked the beginning of the new year. These two periods were further divided by the quarter-days of Imbolg, the first of February, and Lughnasadh, "the commemoration of Lugh," on the first of August.

The feast of Samhain was above all the most important date in the Celtic calendar, and it features many times in mythology. The Celts believed that the duration of the festival was a special mystical time, an interstice between two distinct temporal periods during which the normal order of the universe is suspended and the barriers between the natural and supernatural worlds are removed. All the gods and the dead move freely among the living, sometimes interfering with their affairs. Not surprisingly, the Celts associated many of their greatest mythic events to the feast of Samhain: famous kings and heroes die, and the legendary battle of Magh Tuiredh is supposed to have taken place at this time.

As well as celebrating specific important feast-days, the Celts also marked out certain other times during the year. At the end of the nineteenth century, archeologists found a Celtic calendar inscribed on a sheet of bronze and dating from the early first century AD or the late first century BC. The calendar appears

four druids would chant an incantation over him and he would see in his sleep the future king. Perhaps the best known of all the Celtic prophets was Brighid, who was also expert in poetry, magic, and divination, probably an inheritance from her father Daghdha.

## THE CELTIC RELIGIOUS CALENDAR
Julius Caesar observed that the Gaulish druids' assembly in Carnutes was held at a certain fixed time of the year. The Celts celebrated other religious festivals and rituals at regular times of the year, too. The Celtic religious year revolved around the the seasons and the movements of the sun and the moon, and was divided into two: summer and winter. Summer began on the first of May, after the feast of Beltene on May-Eve. During this festival in

*Above: Bronze boar statuette (Hounslow, Middlesex, England; first century BC to first century AD). The figure was found together with other boars and a wheel, which were perhaps votive offerings to a sun god. Like other Celtic boars, its dorsal spine is emphasized: the animal was a symbol of virility, which was signified in myth and reality by the warrior's bristling hair.*

to have been drawn up by druids, who gave each separate month, and even individual days, the abbreviation *mat*, "good," or *anm*, "not good." This practice accords with the role traditionally attributed to the druids in Celtic mythology of deciding whether a particular day is a good time or not for taking up arms or for being born into the world. According to the Roman writer Pliny the Elder, once a month, on the sixth day of the moon, the druids climbed a sacred oak and cut off the mistletoe with a golden sickle; two bulls were also sacrificed at the same time.

## CELTIC RELIGIOUS SITES AND RITUALS

The Celts worshiped their gods and goddesses in many ways. On one level, they carved wooden, stone, or bronze representations of their deities or sacred animals, such as boars and bulls. They would then worship these carvings or give them as an offering to the gods. On another level, they carried out elaborate and often bizarre rituals and ceremonies at holy places and shrines, some conducted solely by druids, others by the whole tribe. The Celts seem to have had many of these shrines: The Celtic word *nemeton*, meaning "a sacred place," appears in place-names all over the Celtic world. Most of the Celts'

*Left: Madron Well, Cornwall, England. Sources of water were revered by the Celts for their religious powers, and many of these sacred springs and wells continued to be visited for spiritual healing in the Christian era, often dedicated to saints. Madron was also a site of a baptistry. Sick people still drink these waters and hang votive rags on the surrounding trees.*

divinities represented the elemental forces of nature, and according to classical writers Celtic shrines tended to be in secluded groves. Depending on which god or gods were being worshiped, these were either in the depths of forests, in peat bogs, on small, uninhabited islands, on the peaks of mountains, or at other special sites.

Although absolute evidence is lacking, druidic rituals probably also took place at pre-Celtic monuments such as standing stones. Many of these stones, some of which stand singly, in lines, or in circles, had been erected by earlier civilizations to mark boundaries or burial places, but they were often misinterpreted, mythologized, and revered by the Celts as sacred topographical "focuses" of worship. The famous stone circle at Stonehenge in the south of England could have been one such center. The Celts used these prehistoric stones in various ways. Some stones were used to swear oaths, while others were used in healing and fertility rites. Other stones were claimed to have far more incredible properties. According to Irish legend, on the Hill of Tara in County Meath, the mystical center of Ireland, stood the Stone of Fál, a "stone penis" that cried out when it came into contact with the man destined to be king. Tara was the scene of the ritual of the marriage-feast, the *Feis Temhra*, by which the status of the new king was confirmed and his union with his kingdom solemnized. Other legendary stones were used in the ritual selection of Celtic kings, too. One of the several ordeals to test a candidate's fitness for the crown involved

*Right: Spring nymphs from the Roman fort at High Rochester, Northumberland, England (stone relief sculpture; third century AD). Many dedications to a Celtic water deity named Coventina have been found in northern England. This relief may portray a Roman goddess (Venus or Diana, disturbed while bathing) or it could also represent Coventina: classical iconography was often borrowed for Celtic deities. The original context is not known: it was reused in a water-tank at the fort.*

*Left: A late Bronze-Age sacrificial well at Moen, Denmark (c. 800–400 BC). The stylistic similarities in the art of non-Celtic northern Europe points to cultural connections during the Bronze Age. The well held votive bronze vessels and ornaments as well as animal sacrifices. There were also remains of joints of meat in an alder trunk.*

two sacred stones, with just a hand's width between them, which opened up to allow the chosen candidate's chariot to pass through.

The most important sacred places for the Celts were those near water. They saw water as a supernatural dwelling, where gods, giants, and monsters all lived, and from where they occasionally emerged. Throughout the Celtic world, archeologists have found remains of religious activity near wells, springs, streams, rivers, and lakes. In the north

of England, for example, there are many dedications and stone carvings near wells in honor of a Celtic water deity named Coventina. Although we can not be certain of what forms the religious ceremonies took at these sites, the discovery of large ornamental bronze horns suggests that music may have played a part in Celtic rituals. We do know, however, that the Celts threw many different objects into the waters as offerings to the gods. Bronze helmets and shields, stone carvings,

*Above: Lead defixio (curse tablet) from Roman baths (Bath, England; first to second centuries AD). Curses were written in Latin onto lead strips that were rolled up and thrown into the spring waters; the curses invoke the goddess Sulis to bring harm to a personal enemy. Thus the Celtic goddess was believed to have a harmful as well as healing powers.*

*Above right: Pewter mask from culvert of Roman baths (Bath, England; first century AD) This may have been the face mask of a priest or priestess, held in front of the face during rituals.*

and animal sacrifices have been recovered from a number of sites, including the Thames River at Wandsworth, London, and the Witham River near Lincoln, northern England. Several sacrificial wells containing similar items have been discovered in Denmark, while a collection of wooden sculptures have been found in marshes at the mouth of the Seine River in France. These not only included animals and whole human figures, both male and female, but also torsos, heads, limbs, and even internal organs. The goddess of the source, Sequana, from whom the river's name is derived, was associated with healing, and these sculptures were probably

*ex voto* offerings to the deity. Objects were also thrown into springs to invoke the gods to bring harm to an individual. In Bath, southwest England, for example, curses were written on lead tablets and thrown as an offering to the water goddess Sulis.

The Celts also offered more valuable and ornate objects to the gods. Earlier this century, a decorated bronze pony cap was found in a drained lake in Kircudbrightshire, Scotland, while a miniature golden boat has been discovered in County Derry, Ireland. In 1891, a large silver-plated copper bowl was found in a peat bog at Gundestrup, Denmark. The bowl, probably dating to the first or second century BC, is richly decorated on the outside with unidentified deities and on the inside by mythological scenes. It was probably a cult cauldron used by a druid as a ritual vessel in which to mix potions. Cauldrons were very important to druidic religion, and they are frequently mentioned in Celtic mythology. In Irish legend, for example, the cauldron was the attribute of the druid-god Daghdha. Cauldrons have been uncovered at a number of religious sites. One such container, found in a bog at Brå, Jutland, and dating from the third century BC, had been deliberately smashed before being offered to the gods. Another, found at Rynkeby, Denmark, but thought to be Gaulish in origin, was decorated with heads of oxen, perhaps signifying its use as a ritual vessel in animal sacrifice.

Most of the Celts' sacred sites have now disappeared, and our knowledge of ritual activities is mainly limited to the monumental religious sanctuaries of the Roman period. From that time onward, the Celts built more permanent places in which to worship. At Maiden Castle in Dorset, England, for example, the Celts built a circular timber temple in the first century AD, after the Romans had stormed a fort on the site. In the fourth century the temple was rebuilt as a stone building. Archeological excavations in the late 1970s revealed that a similar temple once existed at Hayling Island in Hampshire, England. This building, which had been oriented toward the rising sun, was surrounded by pig and sheep bones, Celtic coins, horse equipment, and weapons. Contemporary literary sources help explain these discoveries. Caesar tells us that the Celts in Gaul used to bring piles of booty from the battlefield to

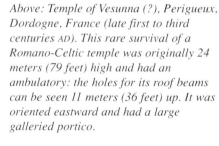

*Above: Temple of Vesunna (?), Perigueux, Dordogne, France (late first to third centuries AD). This rare survival of a Romano-Celtic temple was originally 24 meters (79 feet) high and had an ambulatory: the holes for its roof beams can be seen 11 meters (36 feet) up. It was oriented eastward and had a large galleried portico.*

*Left: Aerial photograph of Romano-Celtic temple site, Hayling Island, Hampshire, England. The rectangular boundary and circular temple were clearly visible as crop-marks during the severe drought of 1976. Many other British sites were revealed by the dry weather that year.*

*Above: Reconstructed portal to a Celtic shrine (Roquepertuse, Bouches-du-Rhône, France; third to second centuries BC). Niches in the columns contained the human skulls of fit young men, probably head-hunted in battle. Diodorus refers to the Celtic custom of warriors taking heads as proof of valor, and such heads were sometimes offered to the gods.*

*Left: Head of Coriosolites (bronze coin from Britanny; first century BC). This Gallic coin depicts a local god, with fashionable Celtic warrior hairstyle: note the chain with a severed head attached hanging from his hair.*

*Above: Maponus head from Northumberland, England (c. second to fourth centuries AD). The stone head has a hollow carved in its crown for libations. Maponus was the divine Youth of northern Britain.*

*Above: Neolithic burial cairns in the Loughcrew Hills, County Meath Ireland (c. 2500–2000 BC). Most of the prehistoric graves that we see today have had their original earth mounds weathered away. These well-preserved examples allow us to understand the frequent mythological Celtic view of them as "fairy castles."*

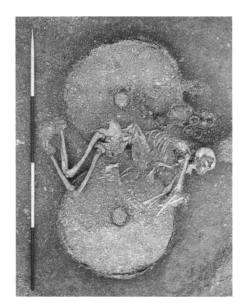

*Above right: Chariot-burial of young adult female, Wetwang, Yorkshire, England (c. second to first centuries BC). A square barrow marked the grave. The wheels and shaft can be seen alongside bronze female goods, including a mirror and work-box; a side of pork, often mentioned in mythology as the "champion's joint," was included for the underworld meal. A similar male burial was found nearby, his Celtic warrior status signified by sword, spears, and shield.*

their sacred places, where they would dedicate them to a war god and accompany the ritual with animal sacrifice.

Recent archeology has provided evidence to support statements made by Greek and Roman writers that the Celts practiced human sacrifice. Excavation in the 1980s of a sacred Gallic site at Ribemont in Picardy, France, revealed pits filled with human bones, the thigh bones purposefully arranged into right-angled patterns. The body of "Lindow Man" recently discovered in peat bog in Cheshire, north England, (now in the British Museum in London) might also have been the victim of druidic sacrifice. According to a number of Roman commentators, the Celts performed several kinds of human sacrifices to appease different gods. The victims of the god Teutates were drowned by being plunged head first into a vat of water, a scene pictured on the Gundestrup cauldron. The victims of Esus were suspended from trees and ritually wounded. The victims of Taranis were burned, several at a time, in large wooden cages.

Classical writers also record that the Celts venerated the human head, and that they would often cut off the heads of their slain enemies and take them home as battle-prizes. However, severed heads were no mere trophies. The Celts believed that they were sacred, that they contained magical properties and that they were a source of beneficial energy. They functioned as a symbol of the divine and the supernatural, warding off evil from the individual and the tribe. They was also associated with healing, fertility, youth and prosperity. The Celts sometimes offered heads of the enemy to warrior-gods, occasionally building entire shrines devoted to skull worship. Stone carved heads probably had similar ritual significance. Some

were hollowed out to hold healing libations. Celtic coins have been found with images of gods wearing severed heads dangling on chains around their necks.

### LIFE AFTER DEATH

It is certain from classical literature, Celtic mythology, and archeological discoveries that the Celts believed in a life after death. Caesar, like virtually every classical writer, claimed that this belief was part of a druid's formal training. However, classical sources disagree over what the Celts believed happened to a person when they died. According to some, the druids taught that a human soul passed from one body to another, a theory that seems to accord with the numerous instances in Irish and Welsh mythology of shape-shifting, of people changing form. Lucan, however, claims that the druids taught that souls continue to control their bodies in another world. Therefore, Lucan adds, the Celts accept death without fear or trepidation since it is a just a stage in a long life. This belief helps explain the Celtic practice of burying the dead along with personal belongings. Chieftains, hero warriors, and other important figures in the tribe were often buried resting on or beside his or her chariot. Graves of warriors also contained the hero's sword, spears, and shield, while women were usually buried with mirrors, work-boxes, and jewelry. Sometimes, the dead were even buried with a side of pork, often mentioned in Celtic mythology as the champion's joint, to sustain them in the Otherworld.

To the Celts, this Otherworld was a vague concept which encompassed a number of coexisting regions representing different aspects of the supernatural kingdom. In Irish mythology, this kingdom not only includes the House of Donn, where all the Irish are said to go after death, but also the happy lands inhabited by Daghdha and the other Tuatha de Danaan gods. After their defeat at the hands of the Sons of Míl, it was decided that Ireland would be divided in two, with the lower half going to the Tuatha de Danaan and the upper half going to the descendants of the Sons of Míl, the Gaels. The Tuatha de Danaan accordingly went underground and Daghdha assigned to each of the chiefs one of the sidhs, or "fairy mounds," that are scattered across the surface of the countryside. Until very recently, these mounds were still regarded as

the dwelling places of the fairy people. According to legend, the Cave of Cruachu, a narrow fissure in a limestone formation near Ráth Cruachan in County Roscommon, gives access to the Otherworld. Irish myths are full of tales of fearsome beasts issuing from the hole to ravage the country.

The Celtic Otherworld is not the gloomy, dark underworld of classical mythology. Instead, it is described as a land where sickness and decay are unknown, a land of innocence where the pleasures of love are untainted by guilt. Its women are so numerous and so lovely that it is sometimes known as *Tir inna*

*Left: Handle of bronze bowl, Hallstatt, Austria (sixth century BC). An early example of Celtic metalwork. The myths abound with descriptions of such fine metal vessels at aristocratic banquets. The cow and the calf are solid cast bronze and are depicted in a geometric style typical of Hallstatt art.*

*mBan*, "The Land of Women." It is filled with enchanting music, and has an abundance of fine food and drink. It is seen as a land of peace of harmony, although this does not mean that its inhabitants forego the main diversion of a heroic society, namely fighting. Their internal conflicts are normally resolved by the intervention of a human being. For example, in the Welsh collection of the *Mabinogion*, Pwyll, Prince of Dyfed, is called upon to descend into Annwn (the Otherworld) to defeat an enemy of King Arawn's. The king takes Pwyll's place in the natural world without anyone noticing, a perfectly fluid intermingling of the supernatural and natural realms.

This perfect fluidity is perhaps the principal feature of all Celtic mythology. Tales and stories proliferate in endless narrative variants, the same gods and goddesses have many different names, powers, and functions, humans and deities seamlessly change places, single characters appear in several different tales under many various guises, and all kinds of creatures constantly change form at will. And yet with all this variety, the underlying concepts of the stories remain more or less constant across the Celtic world. It is this ability to combine diversity with unity that has made the myths and beliefs of the Celts some of the richest and most enchanting of all time.

*Left: "A Spirit or a Sidhe in a Landscape" (oil on board by George William Russell, 1867–1935). The Irish artist's play* Dierdre *was performed in Dublin in 1902, and he is best known as a poet of works based on Celtic mythology. As a painter he tended to concentrate on a particular theme during a particular period. Between 1900 and 1905 he produced a series of images of Celtic spirits in landscape settings.*